YOUNG OBSERVER
TIGER SHARKS
and other dangerous animals

Anita Ganeri

Kingfisher

NEW YORK

KINGFISHER
Larousse Kingfisher Chambers Inc.
95 Madison Avenue
New York, New York 10016

First American edition 1995
10 9 8 7 6 5 4 3 2

LIBRARY OF CONGRESS CATALOGING-IN-
PUBLICATION DATA
Ganeri, Anita -
Tiger sharks and other dangerous
animals/Anita Ganeri.
1st American ed.
p. cm.—(Young Observer)
Includes bibliographical references
and index.
1. Dangerous animals—Miscellanea
—Juvenile literature. [1. Dangerous
animals—Miscellanea.]
I. Title. II. Series.
QL100. G32 1995
591.B'5—dc20 95-6103
CIP AC

ISBN 1-85697-576-2
Printed in Hong Kong

Conceived and created by

David West • CHILDREN'S BOOKS

Author: Anita Ganeri
Consultants: Michael Chinery,
  Alistair Gray, Brian Ward
Cover illustrations: Stephen McLean
  (John Martin and Artists) and
  Rob Shone
Illustrations: David Marshall (Simon
  Girling & associates); James
  Macdonald; Liz Sawyer (Simon
  Girling & associates); Andrew
  Tewson (Simon Girling &
  associates)
Line illustrations: Rob Shone

CONTENTS

INTRODUCTION

Some newspapers are full of blood-curdling stories about people being swallowed by snakes, sliced in two by sharks, and struck down by terrible diseases spread by fleas and flies. But don't be too alarmed—most animals are shy and retiring, and far prefer the quiet life—they move into action only if they feel threatened. Some animals do use their poison to kill the creatures they eat, though. This can lead to problems—especially if they mistake your arm or leg for a juicy snack. What's the best thing to do if you bump into a poisonous animal? Stay calm—and move slowly, but surely, away!

There are dozens of fascinating facts in this book. You can test what you've read—and some of what you may already know—with the Young Observer trivia quiz at the end of each chapter. If you get stuck, the answers are in the back.

CHAPTER ONE

POISONOUS ANIMALS

What do snakes, spiders, scorpions, jellyfish, octopuses, stonefish, stingrays, centipedes, ants, wasps, and bees have in common? They are all poisonous, that's what!

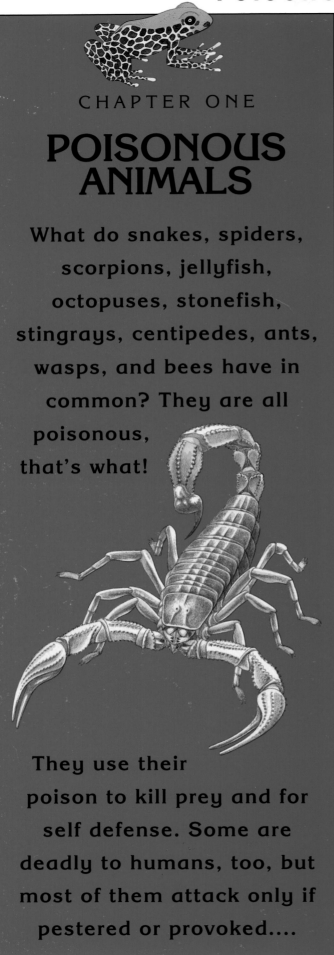

They use their poison to kill prey and for self defense. Some are deadly to humans, too, but most of them attack only if pestered or provoked....

SPIDERS are meat-eaters that feed mainly on insects. They hunt for their **prey** or trap it in silken webs. Then they use poison to kill it—sinking in sharp **fangs** and pumping in the poison. All spiders bite, but only a few put people in peril.

Fang

BLACK WIDOWS (*below*) or redbacks are small, dark, and deadly, and can kill with a single bite if you disturb a web. The problem is, they like to spin webs across toilet seats. Ouch!

THE FUNNEL-WEB SPIDER

(*right*) is bigger, hairier, and far more deadly than the black widow—a bite from a funnel-web can kill you within 2 hours. First you get aches and pains, and you start to sweat. Then you turn blue and froth at the mouth. Death follows unless you can get to the **antivenin** in time.

A funnel-web spider rears up ready to attack!

BIRD-EATING SPIDERS are even bigger! The largest lives in the South American jungle. It's the size of a dinner plate, as you can see in the picture (*left*). These big spiders are peace-loving—unless disturbed. Then they rear up and strike. This is bad news if you're a juicy lizard or bird. The bite hurts, but fortunately is rarely **fatal** to humans.

TARANTULAS (*right*) live in burrows and chase their prey until they catch them! These spiders look fierce and they have a strong bite, but they rarely attack humans. Some are even kept as pets —though your parents may not like the idea!

THE OCEANS ARE HOME to some extremely poisonous creatures, and jellyfish are doubly dangerous because they are so hard to spot in the water. Very few kinds of jellyfish kill, but many give nasty stings. The long, trailing *tentacles* of the Portuguese man-of-war or bluebottle (*left*) are usually used to poison passing prey, such as small fish or shrimps. But not always! *You* are likely to escape with a nasty burning sting. A soup of dried tentacles was once used in a murder attempt—it wasn't successful!

The arm-span of the largest octopuses can be greater than 8 feet, with enough suction power to tug you into the sea. Struggling makes the octopus tighten its grip—stay still, and it will soon lose interest!

THE BLUE-RINGED OCTOPUS (*below*) is just 4 inches across, but it kills more people each year than sharks do. Its *saliva* is poisonous and can enter your blood if it bites you with its parrotlike beak. This tiny octopus is very shy, though, and only attacks when picked up and peered at.

Blue-ringed octopus

6

THE LIONFISH's stripy fins (*left*) hide its secret weapons. This colorful fish is armed with lots of sharp spines for injecting poison into an attacker. Lionfish do sting humans, but the poison rarely kills. In fact, in some countries people eat this fish as a treat. BUT, *be warned*! Before you start to cook a lionfish, remove *all* of its spines. Even a dead lionfish will sting you.

EVERYTHING but the flesh of the death puffer fish (*right*) is deadly poisonous and can kill you in minutes—its heart, liver, skin, bones, and guts. In Japan, raw death puffer is a great delicacy. Called *fugu*, it is served in special restaurants by chefs trained in removing the risky bits. Good eyesight is a must for the job!

*Despite everything, as many as 20 people die of fugu poisoning each year. There is no **antidote**. One Japanese "remedy" is to bury victims up to their necks in mud.*

SOME OF THE MOST POISONOUS SNAKES live in the sea. The trouble is, their bite is painless and their poison slow to act—you might not realize you've been nipped until it's too late. Luckily, sea snakes prefer to leave people in peace and concentrate on fish!

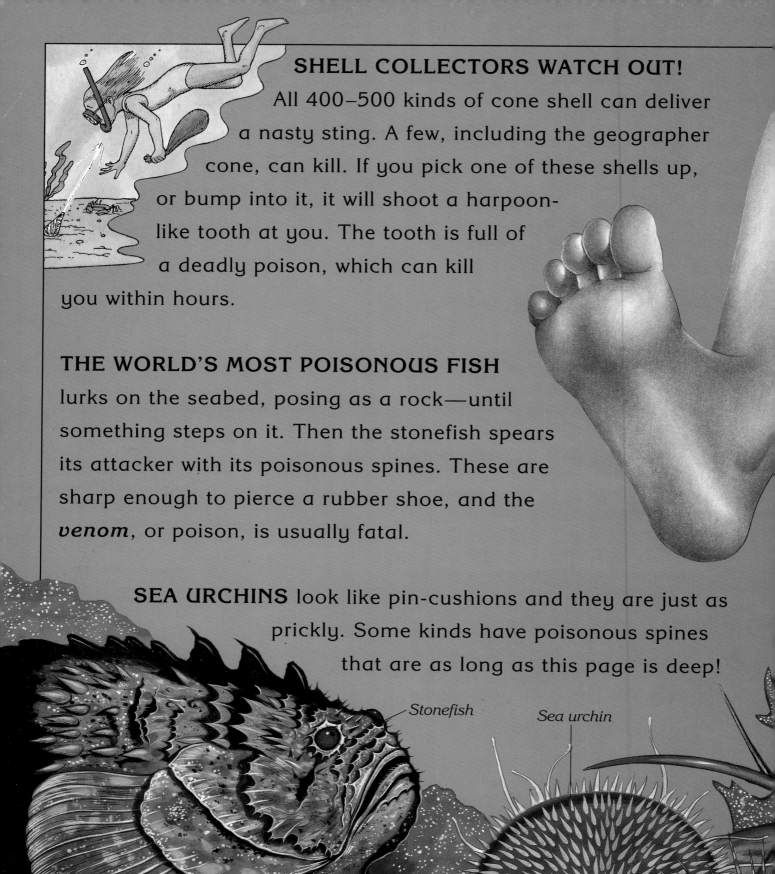

SHELL COLLECTORS WATCH OUT!

All 400–500 kinds of cone shell can deliver a nasty sting. A few, including the geographer cone, can kill. If you pick one of these shells up, or bump into it, it will shoot a harpoon-like tooth at you. The tooth is full of a deadly poison, which can kill you within hours.

THE WORLD'S MOST POISONOUS FISH

lurks on the seabed, posing as a rock—until something steps on it. Then the stonefish spears its attacker with its poisonous spines. These are sharp enough to pierce a rubber shoe, and the *venom*, or poison, is usually fatal.

SEA URCHINS look like pin-cushions and they are just as prickly. Some kinds have poisonous spines that are as long as this page is deep!

Stonefish

Sea urchin

8

STARGAZER FISH are only about 12 inches long, but they pack a powerful punch—they can give off electric shocks *and* they have poisonous spines!

Stargazer

DON'T STEP ON A STINGRAY!

The long thin spike on its tail is poisonous, needle-sharp, and armed with tiny barbs. To fend off an attacker, a stingray whips its tail around and impales its victim on the spike. Stingrays don't usually harm people—unless you annoy them, of course!

CROWN-OF-THORNS STARFISH are armed with sword-like spines, and a cut can sting for days. The starfish are far more deadly to coral than people—they have munched their way through large areas of Australia's Great Barrier Reef.

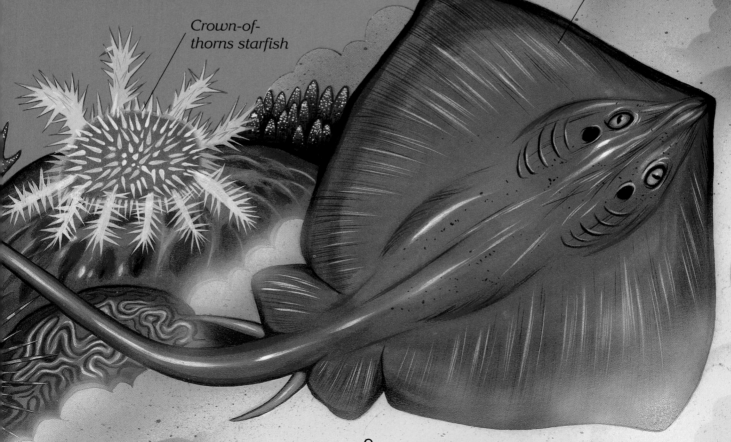

Crown-of-thorns starfish

Stingray

*Spider-hunting wasps (often called tarantula hawks) use their stings to **paralyze** their victim. Then they bury the spider and lay eggs on it. When the grubs hatch, a spider-meat feast is waiting!*

WASPS AND BEES ARE STRIPED

yellow and black for a very good reason—the colors warn that they sting. Some people are **allergic** to the poison in these insects' stings, and can die if they aren't given an antidote. Whatever you do, don't panic if one comes near you—it will probably buzz away if you stand still and leave it alone.

MOST BEES are peaceful creatures, but not all! In Brazil there's a kind of honeybee that attacks in large **swarms**, completely without warning. Once, the Brazilian government even had to send in soldiers armed with flame-throwers to deal with a killer bee attack on a school playground.

Bumblebee

Honeybee

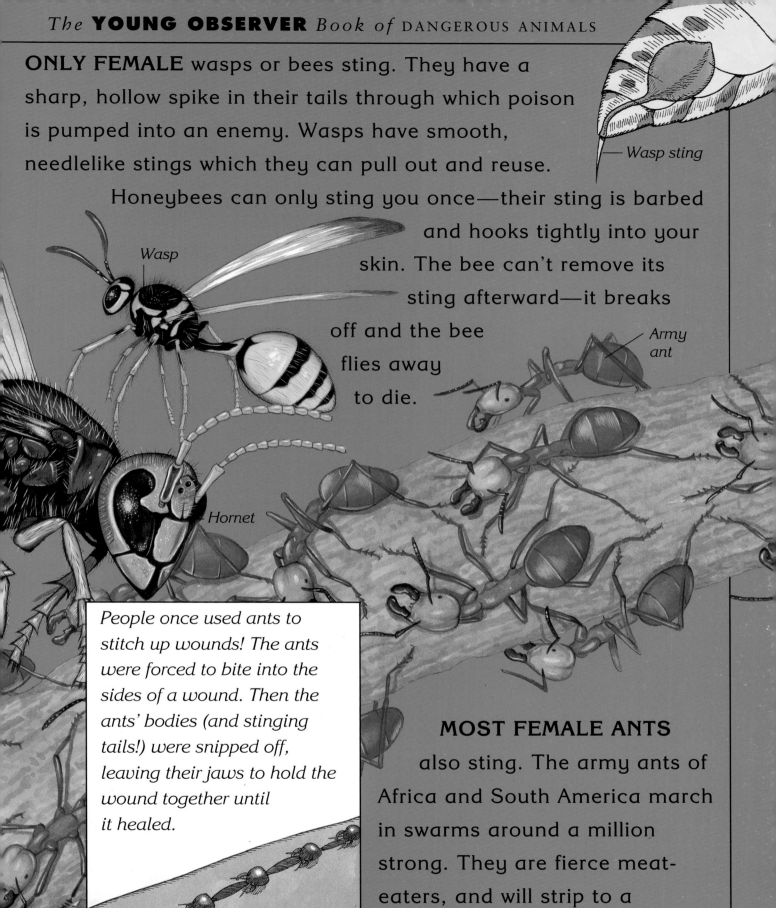

Wasp sting

ONLY FEMALE wasps or bees sting. They have a sharp, hollow spike in their tails through which poison is pumped into an enemy. Wasps have smooth, needlelike stings which they can pull out and reuse.

Honeybees can only sting you once—their sting is barbed and hooks tightly into your skin. The bee can't remove its sting afterward—it breaks off and the bee flies away to die.

Wasp

Hornet

Army ant

People once used ants to stitch up wounds! The ants were forced to bite into the sides of a wound. Then the ants' bodies (and stinging tails!) were snipped off, leaving their jaws to hold the wound together until it healed.

MOST FEMALE ANTS also sting. The army ants of Africa and South America march in swarms around a million strong. They are fierce meat-eaters, and will strip to a skeleton anything that cannot escape their path!

CENTIPEDES (*right*) **ARE MEAT-EATERS** and their first pair of legs is *modified* into fangs which can be used to inject prey with poison. Most centipedes are too small to be dangerous to people, but in Central and South America there are kinds that grow to 12 inches in length. If handled, these insects can give agonizingly painful bites—which sometimes kill.

POISON-ARROW FROGS also live in Central and South America. These tiny creatures have a deadly poison in their brightly colored skins. Local people extract the poison by roasting the frogs over a fire, and then use it to tip their hunting arrows and blowpipe darts. If it gets into the bloodstream, a single drop can kill a large monkey, a small jaguar, or even a human. The poison works by *paralyzing* the muscles—causing death by *suffocation*.

Shrews have sharp teeth and can give nasty bites. The American short-tailed shrew uses its poisonous saliva to help kill its prey. It's strong enough to kill frogs and fish, but wouldn't do you any harm!

Poison-arrow frogs

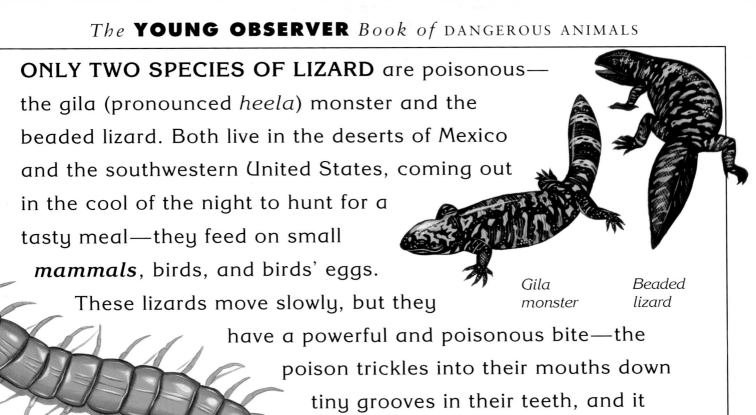

ONLY TWO SPECIES OF LIZARD are poisonous—the gila (pronounced *heela*) monster and the beaded lizard. Both live in the deserts of Mexico and the southwestern United States, coming out in the cool of the night to hunt for a tasty meal—they feed on small **mammals**, birds, and birds' eggs. These lizards move slowly, but they have a powerful and poisonous bite—the poison trickles into their mouths down tiny grooves in their teeth, and it causes pain, numbness and breathing difficulties, heart problems, and eventually death. Fortunately, very few people are ever bitten. The main problem if you are bitten is not so much the poison, but that the lizard refuses to let go!

Gila
monster

Beaded
lizard

Indonesia's Komodo dragon feeds on monkeys, pigs, and deer and is the largest living lizard—males can grow to be 10 feet long (bigger than a car). It isn't poisonous, but its mouth is so full of germs that if its bite doesn't kill you, an infection may carry you off instead!

AROUND 300 SPECIES OF SNAKE are poisonous, but only some are deadly to humans—even so, 30–40,000 people are killed by snakes each year.

In most snakes, the poison fangs are in the front of their mouths and cannot be moved. But some snakes, including vipers, have fangs that fold back when not in use, then swing forward for a lightning-fast strike.

Fang

THE FER-DE-LANCE of *tropical* America (*right*) has long fangs and a lethal bite. In some places, it is called the 4-minute snake, because this is how long its victims take to die!

Hannibal was a famous Roman general who lived over 2,200 years ago and may have owed some of his success to poisonous snakes. According to legend, he once won a sea battle by throwing jars of live snakes at the enemy ships!

AFRICA'S BLACK MAMBA is deadly poisonous—*and* a fast mover. It has a top slithering speed of 10 miles per hour, and is even speedier going downhill.

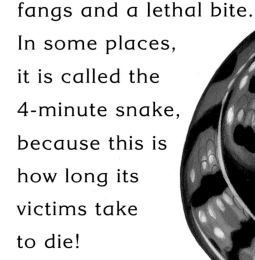

THE BOOMSLANG (*left*) is another deadly African snake. Its fangs are short and at the back of its mouth, and the snake has to chew on its victim's flesh to inject enough poison. If a bite isn't quickly treated with an antivenin, it is usually fatal. The snake is slow to strike, though, and prefers to spend its day hiding in the trees.

Gaboon viper

THE GABOON VIPER's fangs are as long as your little finger—the longest snake fangs of all—but this tropical African snake only swings into action if it is really annoyed. The trouble is, its skin coloring gives it such good *camouflage* among the leaves on the forest floor that you might not notice it until you stepped on it!

BE FAIR TO THE RATTLESNAKE—this American viper does try to warn us. It sounds the alarm by shaking the scaly rattle at the tip of its tail. Woe betide people or animals who ignore the warning, though. If a rattlesnake strikes, the results are often fatal.

A rattle- snake's rattle

COBRAS ARE FAMOUS for their charming ways. In fact, snakes are deaf and cobras cannot hear the snake-charmer's music. When the lid is taken off its basket, the cobra rears up and spreads its hood, ready to strike. It sways from side to side, copying the movement of the snake-charmer's flute, which it views as a potential enemy. Several kinds of cobra live in Africa and Asia, and they are all deadly poisonous. A cobra bite can kill you after 15 minutes of agonizing pain. Some cobras attack by spitting poison into their enemies' eyes, with amazing accuracy.

Some cobras spit their poison.

Ancient "remedies" for snakebites included wearing lucky charms, eating the offending snake, consulting the tribe's snake doctor, and putting gunpowder on the wound and setting it off. None of them is recommended!

The **Young Observer** *Quiz*

1. Which snake pretends to be poisonous?

Is it the:

a) Mole snake?

b) Milk snake?

c) Sea snake?

2. Who keeps bottles of venom?

a) Poisoners?

b) Doctors?

c) Witch doctors?

3. What do people milk snakes for?

a) Milk?

b) Orange juice?

c) Venom?

d) Lots of money?

4. Where do snakes store their poison?

a) In their tails?

b) Inside their bodies?

c) In their heads?

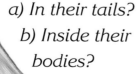

5. How much poison can an arrow-poison frog produce?

a) 500 people?

b) 1,500 people?

c) 2,500 people?

6. Which animal has eight legs and a sting in its tail?

Is it the:

a) Stingray?

b) Spider?

c) Scorpion?

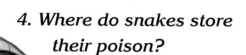

7. What does this poisonous-snake symbol stand for?

a) Medicine? b) Witchcraft?

c) A pet shop?

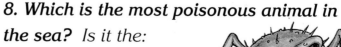

8. Which is the most poisonous animal in the sea? *Is it the:*

a) Stonefish?

b) Box jellyfish?

c) Blue-ringed octopus?

ANSWERS ON PAGES 32–33

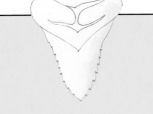

CHAPTER TWO

MAN-EATERS

Terrifying stories are told of tigers, lions, and sharks munching on humans for breakfast. Some animals do eat people—but rest assured, it's rare!

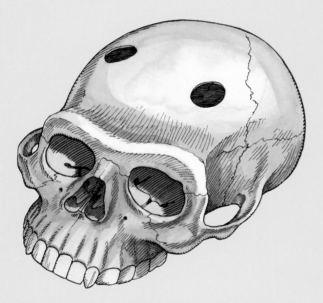

People-eating is not new in the animal kingdom. Thousands of years ago, the owner of this skull lost a tussle with a saber-toothed tiger!

LIONS HUNT in groups and the females usually do the killing. They rarely attack people, but an old or sick lion that cannot catch its usual prey may.

A Roman's idea of a good day out was to go to the Colosseum to watch gladiators fighting for their lives against a range of wild animals, including lions.

One story about man-eaters dates back to the late 1800s, when work on an African railroad line had to be stopped because a pair of lions had eaten so many of the workers.

TIGERS ARE POWERFUL KILLING

machines, but they usually have to be hungry to eat people. There are some, however, that seem to get a taste for human flesh. In India, people who live near tiger *reserves* have various ways of protecting themselves. Tigers often attack from behind, so the man above left is wearing a mask on the back of his head to confuse them.

Rangers wear armor when on patrol in tiger reserves.

THE MAN-EATING

record is held by a tigress that lived in the Himalayan kingdom of Nepal in the early 1900s. She is said to have eaten 438 people in just 8 years.

PEOPLE HAVE LONG HUNTED TIGERS for sport

or for profit. There were as many as 100,000 wild Asian tigers in the year 1900. So many have been killed that they could be virtually *extinct* in the wild by the year 2000.

SHARKS have long had a reputation for eating people. In fact, only around 40 out of the 250 species of shark have been known to attack people. And, of those, only about 10 species are killers, taking 100 or so swimmers a year. But sharks do not usually attack without reason. It is thought that they simply mistake humans for large fish or seals, their normal prey.

Black tip shark

Great white shark

Among the odder items found inside a captured shark's stomach are whole suits of armor, ships' anchors, oil drums, car license plates, beer cans, and old tires. One shark had even managed to swallow a porcupine!

THE MOST NOTORIOUS

man-eating fish is the great white shark. Its powerful jaws can bite a person clean in half, and males can grow to measure 20 feet from nose tip to tail. Other dangerous sharks include tiger sharks, blue sharks, makos, and black tip sharks. If in doubt, stay firmly on dry land!

PEARL DIVERS in waters off the Pacific Islands found an unusual way to avoid being attacked by sharks. To give themselves time to hunt for the precious jewels, the divers used to put the sharks into a kind of trance by "kissing" them. This might have worked with a drowsy old nurse shark, but kissing a tiger shark is not to be recommended!

Tiger shark

Blue shark

SWIMMING WITH KILLER SHARKS

is a risky business. If they are studying sharks in the wild, photographers or scientists often work from inside the safety of a metal cage. Others wear special shark-proof suits, called neptunics (*below*). These are made from thousands of steel rings which even a shark's razor-sharp teeth cannot bite through.

But if you don't have a metal cage or a neptunic, you could always try wearing a striped swimsuit—if you are very lucky, any sharks you bump into will mistake you for a deadly poisonous banded sea snake, and leave you alone!

PIRANHAS (right) **HAVE HUGE APPETITES** and strong jaws with razor-sharp, snappy teeth. They live in the rivers of Central and South America, and normally eat other fish, or *carrion*. But if an animal falls into the river, the piranhas attack with lightning speed, stripping it to the bone in minutes. There are reports of piranhas eating people who have fallen out of boats, but the fish usually attack only if there is blood in the water from a wound.

CROCODILES WERE WORSHIPED as gods in ancient Egypt, and mummified when they died. People have also found mummies of crocodile victims, including a girl whose legs had been bitten off. Crocodiles and alligators are still eating people today. Some attacks happen when people step on crocodiles in the water, mistaking them for logs. The logs suddenly turn very nasty and lash out with their huge, snapping jaws and teeth.

BARRACUDAS (*right*) are even more feared than sharks in some parts of the world. You're likely to be attacked if you wear something shiny, or if you try to mingle with a school of fish. Barracudas can also be dangerous when they are dead. They eat any old garbage when they are ill, and this can make their flesh very poisonous to eat.

BOAS AND PYTHONS don't use poison to kill their prey. They coil their bodies around it and squeeze it to death instead. The snakes then swallow their meal whole, and they can gulp down a small antelope. Some even eat children —in Pakistan, a python once swallowed an 8-year-old boy. But an adult human would probably prove too big a mouthful. Its shoulders would stick in the snake's throat!

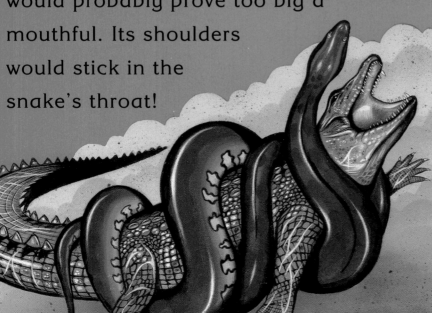

In Norway in 1932, a sea eagle swooped down and carried off a girl playing in her garden. Gripping her in its talons, it flew toward its mountaintop nest, but dropped her on a ledge. She was found later, fast asleep and unharmed.

SOME ANIMALS are dangerous only when you're dead. These are the carrion-eaters, animals that feast on dead and rotting flesh. Vultures (*left*) move quickly to pick a **carcass** clean, sometimes eating so much that they can hardly fly! The bird's head and neck are bare —feathers would get clogged with blood. In the Parsi religion of India, people's bodies are placed on funeral towers so vultures can devour them.

In the past, doctors used maggots to clean infected wounds and try to prevent an illness. The maggots happily ate the pus and rotten flesh around the wound, leaving it to heal cleanly. Just recently, doctors have been looking at this technique and even using it successfully in some cases.

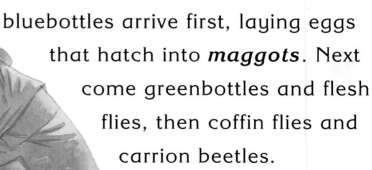

FORENSIC SCIENTISTS can work out when someone died by studying the insects feeding on the rotting body. Different insects move in at different times. Houseflies and bluebottles arrive first, laying eggs that hatch into **maggots**. Next come greenbottles and flesh flies, then coffin flies and carrion beetles.

The **Young Observer** *Quiz*

1. Which explorer was nearly killed by a lion?

a) Livingstone?
b) Stanley?
c) Scott?

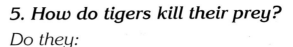
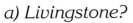

2. Which fish "nails" its prey?

Is it the:
a) Megamouth?
b) Hammerhead shark?
c) Tiger shark?

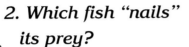

3. Why don't sharks have to brush their teeth?

Because:
a) Their teeth don't decay?
b) Their old teeth are replaced by new ones?
c) They don't get toothache?

4. Which shark is harmless to humans?

Is it the:
a) Tiger shark?
b) Whale shark?
c) Basking shark?

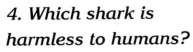

5. How do tigers kill their prey?

Do they:
a) Bite them to death?
b) Claw them to death?
c) Suffocate them?

6. Which reptile is a notorious man-eater?

Is it the:
a) Nile crocodile?
b) Saltwater crocodile?
c) Alligator?

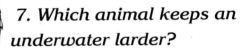

7. Which animal keeps an underwater larder?

Is it the:
a) Crocodile?
b) Shark?
c) Tiger?

8. Which animals have elastic mouths?

Is it:
a) Snakes?
b) Sharks?
c) Frogs?

ANSWERS ON PAGES 34–35

CHAPTER THREE

DISEASE AND PESTILENCE

You don't have to venture into the darkest jungle or the depths of the ocean to come across dangerous creatures. Some of the most harmful animals of all are very common in towns, cities, and homes.

These animals include bats, rats, foxes, fleas, flies, and cockroaches. All can be responsible for spreading disease and pestilence among human beings.

Flea

THE PLAGUE is a terrible disease which, since ancient times, has erupted and swept across Europe, Asia, and Africa, killing millions of people. The Black Death was an outbreak of the plague which is thought to have wiped out a quarter of the population of Europe (about 25 million people) in just four years, 1347–1351— and millions more in Asia.

Plague victims develop boils, then a high fever followed by vomiting and agonizing pain. The nursery rhyme "Ring a ring o' roses" was first sung in London in 1665 during a plague outbreak that killed 70,000 people. The "roses" refer to the red rashes that covered victims' bodies.

BLACK RATS are often blamed for carrying the plague. In fact, they are *hosts* to the real culprits, bloodsucking fleas that live on infected animals—mainly rats, but also squirrels and other animals. If the fleas bite humans to suck their blood, they pass on the infection. Rats act as carriers of several other potentially fatal diseases, including Weil's disease. This illness can cause flu-like symptoms and then make you very ill. It is passed on by rat's urine in water—it's not a good idea to swim in ponds and rivers.

RABIES causes thousands of deaths every year. It is passed to humans by the bite of an infected animal, such as a cat, dog, fox, skunk, raccoon, or vampire bat. Early symptoms are headaches, fever, and a terrible fear of drinking. Rabies is fatal once the symptoms appear. People going to places where rabies is common can be injected with a *vaccine*.

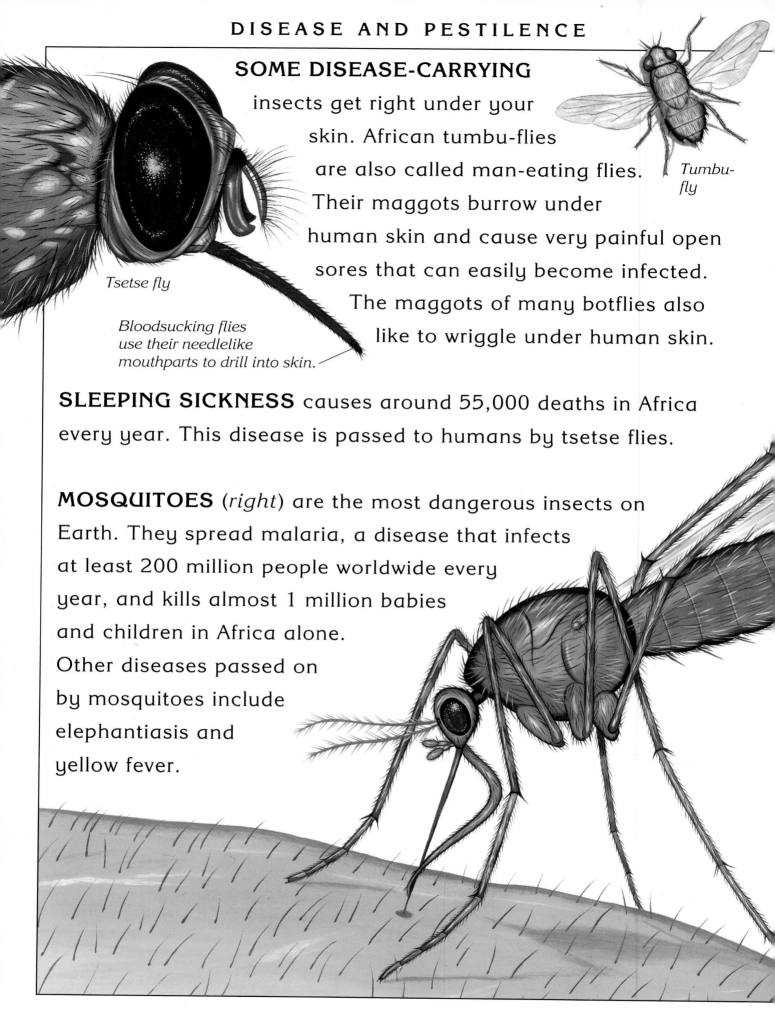

SOME DISEASE-CARRYING

insects get right under your skin. African tumbu-flies are also called man-eating flies. Their maggots burrow under human skin and cause very painful open sores that can easily become infected. The maggots of many botflies also like to wriggle under human skin.

Tumbu-fly

Tsetse fly

Bloodsucking flies use their needlelike mouthparts to drill into skin.

SLEEPING SICKNESS causes around 55,000 deaths in Africa every year. This disease is passed to humans by tsetse flies.

MOSQUITOES (*right*) are the most dangerous insects on Earth. They spread malaria, a disease that infects at least 200 million people worldwide every year, and kills almost 1 million babies and children in Africa alone. Other diseases passed on by mosquitoes include elephantiasis and yellow fever.

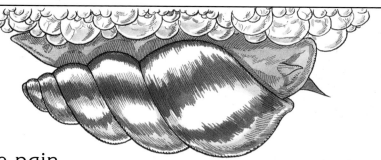

BILHARZIA is a tropical disease that affects around 200 million people and kills about 37,000 every year.

It causes terrible pain, sickness, and diarrhea. Bilharzia is carried by small, *parasitic* worms that live inside freshwater snails (*above right*) for part of their lives. Later the worms swim off into the water, where they enter the skin, and then the bloodstream, of people swimming or washing. There, the male and female worms pair (*left*), mate, and lay millions of eggs.

MITES are tiny parasites that live on plants and animals, sucking out plant juices or body fluids, and even eating scraps of dead skin. Some kinds of mite are useful to us, but others cause diseases such as scabies—an extremely itchy and infectious skin disease caused by the itch mite (*left*) burrowing under the skin.

Ticks are small parasites that are related to mites. They live by sucking blood and spread disease through germs in their saliva when they bite. Ticks may wait for years for a suitable source of food to pass by.

FOR OTHER PESTILENT CREATURES, look no further than your home. Flies carry germs on their feet and in their vomit and droppings, and can spread them to any uncovered food they land on. The humble housefly carries more than 30 diseases—including food poisoning, dysentery, and typhoid.

COCKROACHES (*right*) get everywhere and eat anything! Outdoor species feed on dead animals and fallen fruit. Indoors, cockroaches will head straight for any food or garbage left lying around. They can carry germs on their feet and spread illnesses such as food poisoning.

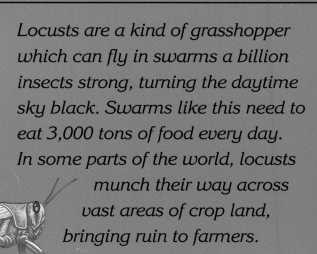

Locusts are a kind of grasshopper which can fly in swarms a billion insects strong, turning the daytime sky black. Swarms like this need to eat 3,000 tons of food every day. In some parts of the world, locusts munch their way across vast areas of crop land, bringing ruin to farmers.

The **Young Observer** *Quiz*

1. Which animal spreads the most disease and death?

Is it the:
a) Cockroach?
b) Rat?
c) Flea?

2. Which insect holds the high-jump record?

Is it the:
a) Fly?
b) Cockroach?
c) Flea?

3. Who saved a town from the Black Death?

Was it the:
a) Ham Piper of Pamelin?
b) Pied Piper of Hamelin?

4. How do tsetse flies transmit disease?

a) By air?
b) Through the blood system?
c) Through the nervous system?

5. Which bloodsucking animal is making a medical comeback?

Is it the:
a) Vampire bat?
b) Leech?
c) Flea?

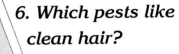

6. Which pests like clean hair?

a) Lice?
b) Mice?
c) Fleas?

7. Which creepy-crawlies may cause asthma?

a) Cat fleas? b) Dust mites?
c) Spiders?

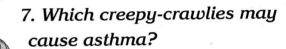
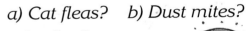

8. Which is the world's most dangerous animal?

Is it the:
a) Piranha?
b) Tiger?
c) Human being?

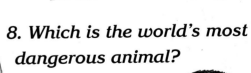

ANSWERS ON PAGES 36–37

The **Answers** to Chapter One (PAGE 17)

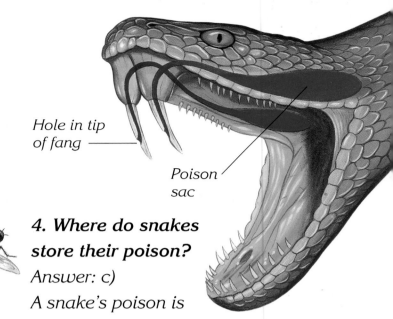

Hole in tip of fang —

Poison sac

1. Which snake pretends to be poisonous?

Answer: b)
In nature, bold colors such as red, black, and yellow warn that an animal is poisonous. The harmless milk snake (left top) fools its enemies because its skin-coloring is similar to that of the deadly coral snake (left below). The hoverfly mimics a wasp in the same way.

2. Who keeps bottles of venom?

Answer: b)
Doctors use snake venom, or poison, to produce medicines called antivenins for treating snakebite victims. Treatment is quickest if you know which snake bit you!

3. Why do people "milk" snakes?

Answer: c)
"Milking" a snake means tricking it into biting something so that its venom can be collected in a jar and used to make antivenins. One South African snake-milker handled 780,000 snakes without being bitten once!

4. Where do snakes store their poison?

Answer: c)
A snake's poison is made by salivary glands inside the snake's mouth and injected through two, long fangs. Each species of snake has its own poison. Some poisons act on the nervous system and stop the heart and lungs working properly. Others either cause fatal blood clots, or prevent blood clotting, so that the victim bleeds to death.

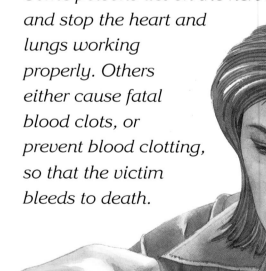

5. How much poison can a poison-arrow frog produce?

Answer: b)

Although so deadly, most poison-arrow frogs are the size of mice, or smaller. One of the deadliest is the golden poison-arrow frog. A single frog has enough poison in its skin to kill nearly 1,500 people. The poison acts quickly, causing paralysis, then death.

6. Which animal has eight legs and a sting in its tail?

Answer: c)

Scorpions have eight legs like their relatives, the spiders, but they keep their poison in a spine in the tip of their tails. To defend itself, or to kill a large spider or insect to eat, a scorpion curls its tail over its head and strikes. Some of the larger species of scorpion are as poisonous as cobras and could easily kill you.

7. What does this poisonous-snake symbol stand for?

Answer: a)

The ancient Greek and Roman god of healing, Aesculapius, was often shown holding a staff with snakes coiled around it. The snake is still used as a symbol of the medical profession today, on journals, books, and clinic signs.

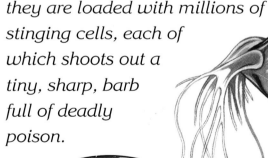

8. Which is the most poisonous animal in the sea?

Answer: b)

The Australian box jellyfish, or sea wasp, can kill you within minutes. Make sure you don't brush against its tentacles—they are loaded with millions of stinging cells, each of which shoots out a tiny, sharp, barb full of deadly poison.

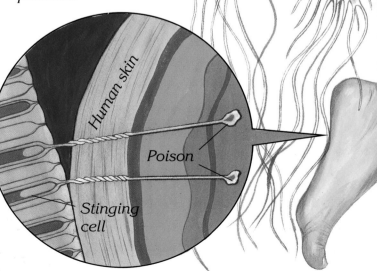

Human skin

Poison

Stinging cell

The **Answers** to Chapter Two (PAGE 25)

1. Which explorer was nearly killed by a lion?

Answer: a)

The famous explorer David Livingstone (1813–1873) was nearly killed by a lion when traveling in Africa. The attack left him with 11 tooth-mark scars and a badly crushed shoulder.

3. Why don't sharks have to brush their teeth?

Answer: b)

A shark has several rows of teeth and keeps on growing new teeth throughout its life. When a tooth wears or falls out, there's always a new one ready to move out to replace it.

Tiger shark

Jaw   New teeth

2. Which fish "nails" its prey?

Answer: b)

The hammerhead shark's extraordinary head is shaped like a hammer, with eyes and nostrils at each end. As the shark swims, it swings its head from side to side. This helps it to track prey by smell. Hammerheads mainly eat fish and shellfish, but they will also charge people in boats, especially if attacked with spears or harpoons.

Whale shark

4. Which shark is harmless to humans?

Answer: b) and c)

The whale shark is the world's biggest fish, reaching over 60 feet in length. Despite its size, it does not attack people. Like the smaller basking shark, it feeds solely on animal plankton.

Basking shark

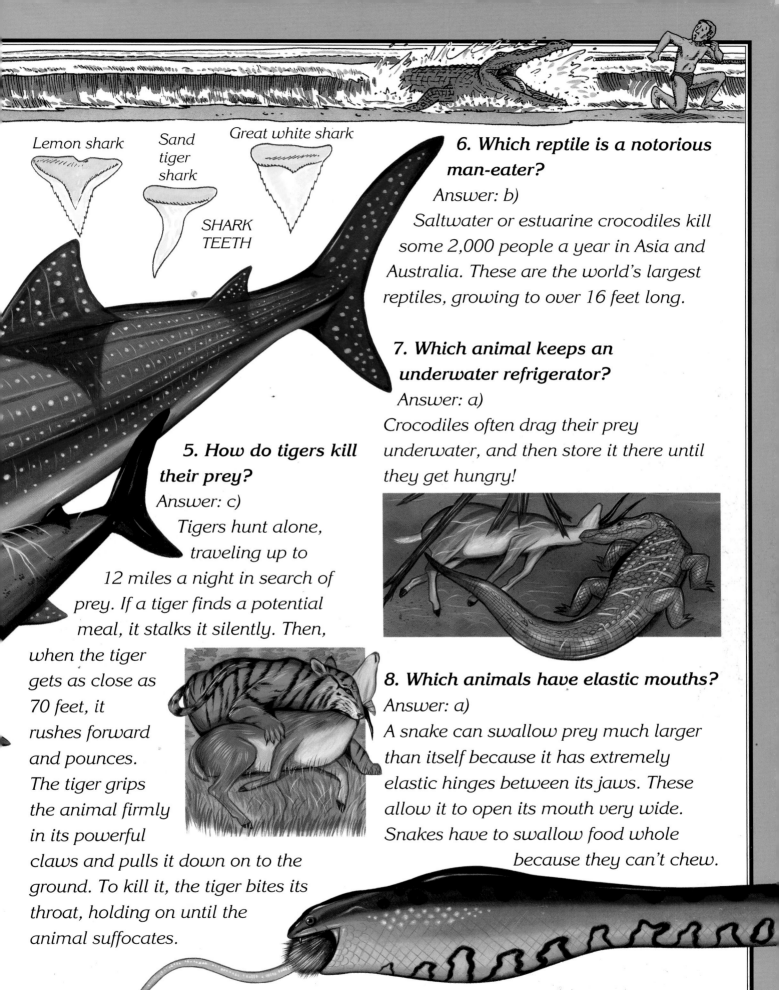

Lemon shark

Sand tiger shark

Great white shark

SHARK TEETH

6. Which reptile is a notorious man-eater?

Answer: b)
Saltwater or estuarine crocodiles kill some 2,000 people a year in Asia and Australia. These are the world's largest reptiles, growing to over 16 feet long.

7. Which animal keeps an underwater refrigerator?

Answer: a)
Crocodiles often drag their prey underwater, and then store it there until they get hungry!

5. How do tigers kill their prey?

Answer: c)
Tigers hunt alone, traveling up to 12 miles a night in search of prey. If a tiger finds a potential meal, it stalks it silently. Then, when the tiger gets as close as 70 feet, it rushes forward and pounces. The tiger grips the animal firmly in its powerful claws and pulls it down on to the ground. To kill it, the tiger bites its throat, holding on until the animal suffocates.

8. Which animals have elastic mouths?

Answer: a)
A snake can swallow prey much larger than itself because it has extremely elastic hinges between its jaws. These allow it to open its mouth very wide. Snakes have to swallow food whole because they can't chew.

The **Answers** to Chapter Three (PAGE 31)

1. Which animals spread the most disease and death?

Answer: b)

Rats can carry many potentially fatal diseases, including Weil's disease, Lassa fever, and rat-bite fever. They are also hosts for the fleas that pass on the plagues that have killed more people than all the wars ever fought, and the fleas and mites that carry kinds of typhus.

2. Which insect holds the high-jump record?

Answer: c)

For its size, the tiny flea can jump higher than any other animal. It can jump 130 times its own height.

Once upon a time, the town of Hamelin in Germany was over-run with rats. There were rats everywhere—in every house and every cupboard. Cats were no use—the rats fought them off. The mayor offered to reward anyone who could get rid of these pests. Rat-catchers came with their traps and their poisons, but nothing worked. Then, one day, a stranger appeared in town and began to play his magic pipe. As he played, rats poured onto the streets and scurried after him. The Piper led them to the river, where they all drowned. The town was free! But the mayor forgot to pay the reward. So the Piper began to play again, and this time all the children began to follow him. He led them out of the town and far away, never to be seen again.

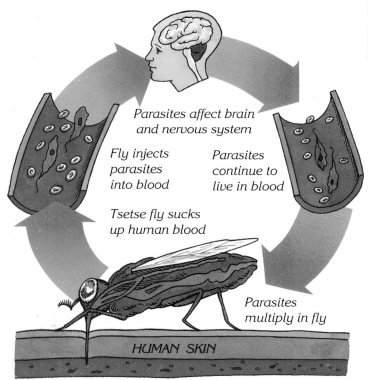

Parasites affect brain and nervous system

Fly injects parasites into blood

Parasites continue to live in blood

Tsetse fly sucks up human blood

Parasites multiply in fly

HUMAN SKIN

3. Who saved a town from the Black Death?

Answer: b (see above)

This story is probably based on the real town of Hamelin and its plague of rats.

4. How do tsetse flies transmit disease?

Answer: b)

When they bite people to suck their blood, tsetse flies pass on the microscopically tiny, single-celled parasites that cause sleeping sickness. This disease starts with

6. Which pests like clean hair?

Answer: a)
Female head lice (right) lay their eggs in clean human hair. The eggs, or nits, hatch into baby lice which make your head itch. You can get rid of them with a special shampoo and comb.

7. Which creepy-crawlies may cause asthma?

Answer: b)
Dust mites (below) live on household dust (which is mostly made up of flakes of dead human skin). Millions of these mites live in your bed. Most people never notice them. When you breathe their tiny droppings, your lungs may react by wheezing. This can lead to allergies or asthma.

8. Which is the world's most dangerous animal?

Answer: c)
The most dangerous animals in the world are not rats or mosquitoes, but human beings! We are one of the few creatures to kill its own kind. We're also the only *living* creatures that deliberately destroy our environment—polluting the land, rivers, and oceans.

fever, headaches and sleepiness. If it isn't treated early, death follows.

5. Which bloodsucking animal is making a medical comeback?

Answer: b)
Medicinal leeches were once widely used by doctors and are now making a comeback. As a leech feeds, it injects a chemical that stops the blood from clotting.

USEFUL WORDS

ALLERGY *A reaction of the body caused by being sensitive to a foreign substance. Some people are allergic to insect stings, for example—the bite may swell up or make their skin break out in a rash. Hay fever is an allergic reaction to plant pollen. Other people are allergic to foods such as milk, wheat, or nuts.*

ANTIDOTE *A medicine or other substance given to stop the harmful effects of a poison.*

ANTIVENIN *A medicine used to treat people who have been bitten by venomous animals, particularly snakes and spiders. Antivenins are made by treating animals with small doses of venom, until their blood produces its own antidote, the antivenin.*

CAMOUFLAGE *A method of disguise. Many animals have built-in camouflage through body color, pattern, or shape, which helps them to blend in with their background and hide from predators.*

CARCASS *The dead body of an animal.*

CARRION *Dead and rotting meat.*

EXTINCTION *When an animal or plant species dies out, and it no longer exists on Earth.*

FANG *Part of an animal's body that is adapted for injecting poison. This may be a tooth (in snakes), or a clawlike fang (in centipedes and spiders).*

FATAL *A fatal illness or accident is one that results in death.*

FORENSIC SCIENTIST *A scientist who helps the police to understand evidence to solve crimes. In murder cases, forensic science is an important means of finding the cause and time of death.*

HOST *See PARASITE.*

MAGGOT *The wormlike young of some flies, especially houseflies.*

MAMMAL *A member of a group of animals which feed their young on milk made in the mother's breast. The group includes humans, cats, dogs, bats, bears, horses, whales, and many other animals.*

MODIFY *To change or alter, usually only slightly.*

NERVOUS SYSTEM *The brain, the spinal cord (the large bundle of nerves that run down the back, enclosed and protected by the backbone), and the nerves that run throughout the body. Nerves carry messages to and from the* brain, so that it can keep vital organs such as the heart and lungs working smoothly. Sensory nerves (touch, taste, hearing, smell, and sight) "tell" the brain what is happening in the world outside the body and allow it to react.

PARALYSIS When an animal cannot move because something is preventing its muscles from working. Paralysis is usually caused by damage to the nervous system.

PARASITE An animal or plant that lives on or in the body of another animal or plant (called the host), obtaining nourishment from it. The host is usually damaged by the presence of a parasite.

PLANKTON Microscopically tiny plants or animals that float on seas or lakes. Plankton are an important food source for many animals, including whales.

PREY Animals that are hunted, killed, and eaten by other animals.

REPTILE A member of a group of animals which includes snakes, lizards, crocodiles, and turtles. Most reptiles have dry, scaly skin and their eggs have leathery skins.

RESERVE A wildlife reserve is an area of land that has been set up to protect plants and animals. The land cannot be cleared for farming, and hunting is banned by law.

SALIVA Another word for spit, the liquid produced in an animal's mouth.

SPECIES A species is an individual kind of plant or animal, such as a gorilla or a koala. All the members of a species look similar and can breed together.

SUFFOCATION When an animal dies from lack of air—its mouth and nose may be blocked, or its breathing muscles may be paralyzed.

SWARM A large group of moving insects, such as bees or locusts.

TENTACLE A long, thin, flexible feeler used for stinging or trapping prey, as well as for sensing things and moving.

TROPICAL A word used to describe the very hot lands near the Equator, or things that live in these regions.

VACCINE A medicine containing a mild dose of the germ that causes a disease, which is injected or swallowed so that the body builds up a resistance to the disease.

VENOM A poisonous liquid that some creatures, including some snakes and spiders, inject in a bite or a sting.

INDEX